Pebble Plus
Bilingüe/Bilingual

ANIMALES AFRICANOS/AFRICAN ANIMALS
Elefantes/Elephants

por/by Sydnie Meltzer Kleinhenz

Traducción/Translation: Dr. Martín Luis Guzmán Ferrer
Editor consultor/Consulting Editor: Dra. Gail Saunders-Smith

Consultor/Consultant: George Wittemyer, PhD
NSF International Postdoctoral Fellow
University of California at Berkeley

Capstone

Mankato, Minnesota

Pebble Plus is published by Capstone Press,
151 Good Counsel Drive, P.O. Box 669, Mankato, Minnesota 56002.
www.capstonepress.com

1 2 3 4 5 6 14 13 12 11 10 09

Library of Congress Cataloging-in-Publication Data
Meltzer Kleinhenz, Sydnie.
   [Elephants. Spanish & English]
   Elefantes = Elephants / por/by Sydnie Meltzer Kleinhenz.
   p. cm. — (Animales africanos = African animals)
   Includes index.
   Summary: "Discusses elephants, their African habitat, food, and behavior — in both English and Spanish" —
Provided by publisher.
   ISBN-13: 978-1-4296-3266-9 (hardcover)
   ISBN-10: 1-4296-3266-6 (hardcover)
   1. Elephants — Africa — Juvenile literature. I. Title. II. Title: Elephants. III. Series.
QL737.P98M4318 2009
599.67 — dc22   2008034543

Editorial Credits
Erika L. Shores, editor; Katy Kudela, bilingual editor; Adalín Torres-Zayas, Spanish copy editor;
   Renée T. Doyle, set designer; Laura Manthe, photo researcher

Photo Credits
Afripics.com, 6–7, 8–9
Digital Vision/Gerry Ellis, 16–17
Dreamstime/Chris Fourie, 10–11; Nicole Kuehl, 20–21
Gary W. Sargent, 5
iStockphoto/Beverly Guhl Davis, 22
Photodisc/Siede Preis, cover, 1, 3 (skin)
Shutterstock/EcoPrint, 18–19; Jody Dingle, 1; Neil Wigmore, 15; Vera Bogaerts, 12–13; Victor Soares, cover

Note to Parents and Teachers

The Animales africanos/African Animals set supports national science standards related
to life science. This book describes and illustrates elephants in both English and Spanish.
The images support early readers in understanding the text. The repetition of words and
phrases helps early readers learn new words. This book also introduces early readers
to subject-specific vocabulary words, which are defined in the Glossary section. Early
readers may need assistance to read some words and to use the Table of Contents,
Glossary, Internet Sites, and Index sections of the book.

Table of Contents

Living in Africa 4

Up Close! 8

Eating and Drinking 14

Staying Safe 20

Glossary 22

Internet Sites 24

Index 24

Tabla de contenidos

La vida en África 4

¡De cerca! 8

Qué comen y beben 14

Estar a salvo 20

Glosario 23

Sitios de Internet 24

Índice 24

Living in Africa

The biggest land animals live in Africa. Elephants roam the grassy savanna.

La vida en África

Los animales terrestres más grandes viven en África. Los elefantes recorren sabanas llenas de pasto.

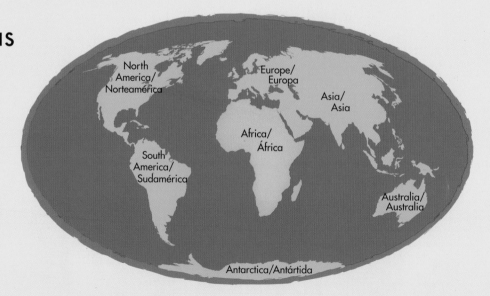

World Map/Mapamundi

The savanna is hot.
Elephants shower themselves
with cool water.

En la sabana hace mucho
calor. Los elefantes se
bañan con agua fresca.

Map of Africa/
Mapa de África

 where elephants live/
lugares donde viven elefantes

Up Close!

Wrinkly elephant skin can get a sunburn. Elephants roll in mud. The mud works like sunscreen.

¡De cerca!

La piel arrugada de los elefantes puede quemarse con el sol. Los elefantes se revuelcan en el lodo. El lodo les sirve de crema para protegerse del sol.

An elephant's trunk is more
than a nose. Elephants play
and give hugs with their trunks.

La trompa del elefante es más
que una nariz. Los elefantes
juegan y se abrazan con
sus trompas.

Elephants grow two jumbo teeth called tusks. Elephants use their tusks to break branches.

A los elefantes les crecen dos dientotes llamados colmillos. Los elefantes usan sus colmillos para romper ramas.

Eating and Drinking

Elephants eat all day.

Their trunks grab branches,

leaves, and grass.

Qué comen y beben

Los elefantes comen todo el día.

Con sus trompas agarran

ramas, hojas y pasto.

Some months are dry
on the savanna.
Elephants must walk far
to find food and water.

Algunos meses son muy secos
en la sabana. Los elefantes
tienen que caminar lejos para
encontrar comida y agua.

Mothers teach calves
to use their trunks.
Calves learn to blow
water into their mouths.

Las madres enseñan a
los bebés a usar sus trompas.
Los elefantitos aprenden a soplar
agua dentro de sus hocicos.

Staying Safe

Calves stay near their mothers.

The herd keeps them safe at night.

Good night, elephants.

Estar a salvo

Los elefantes bebés se quedan

cerca de sus madres. La manada

los tiene a salvo en la noche.

Buenas noches, elefantes.

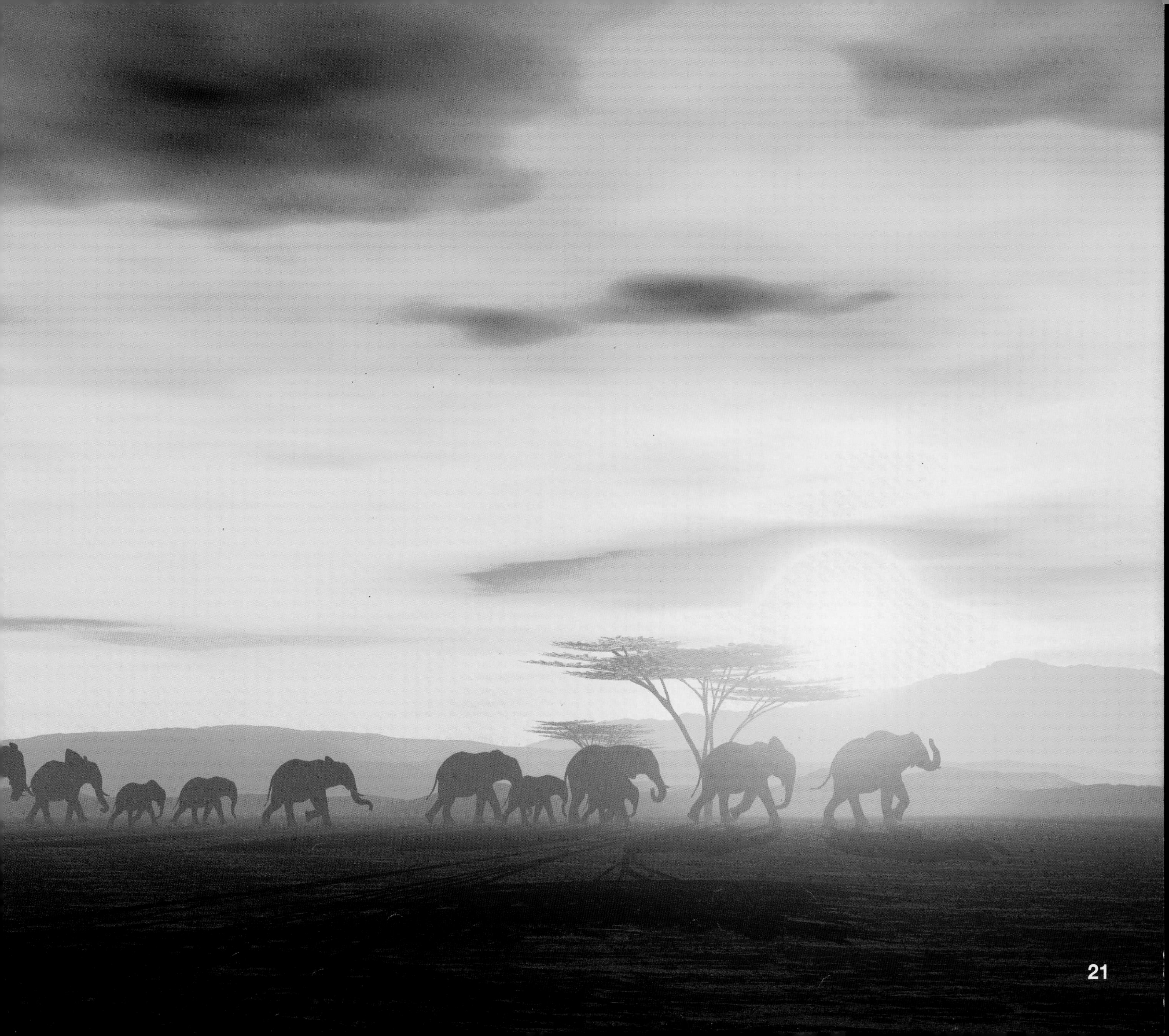

Glossary

herd — a group of elephants; an elephant herd is made up of related female elephants and their young; male elephants live on their own.

roam — to wander

savanna — a flat, grassy plain with few trees

sunburn — sore skin caused by staying in the sun too long

sunscreen — lotion that prevents sunburn

trunk — an elephant's nose; elephants use their trunk like a hand.

tusk — a long, curved, pointed tooth

Glosario

el colmillo — diente largo, curvo y en punta

la crema para el sol — loción que impide quemaduras

la manada — grupo de elefantes; una manada de elefantes se compone de elefantes hembra emparentadas y sus crías; los elefantes macho viven solos.

la quemadura de sol — piel adolorida por estar demasiado en el sol

recorrer — deambular

la sabana — planicie con pasto y pocos árboles

la trompa — la nariz del elefante; los elefantes usan su trompa como mano.

Internet Sites

FactHound offers a safe, fun way to find educator-approved Internet sites related to this book.

Here's what you do:

1. Visit *www.facthound.com*
2. Choose your grade level.
3. Begin your search.

This book's ID number is 9781429632669.

FactHound will fetch the best sites for you!

Index

Africa, 4

food, 14, 16

grass, 4, 14

herds, 20

mothers, 18, 20

mud, 8

night, 20

playing, 10

savanna, 4, 6, 16

skin, 8

sunburn, 8

trunks, 10, 14, 18

tusks, 12

walking, 16

water, 6, 16, 18

Sitios de Internet

FactHound te brinda una forma segura y divertida de encontrar sitios de Internet relacionados con este libro y aprobados por docentes.

Lo haces así:

1. Visita *www.facthound.com*
2. Selecciona tu grado escolar.
3. Comienza tu búsqueda.

El número de identificación de este libro es 9781429632669.

¡FactHound buscará los mejores sitios para ti!

Índice

África, 4

agua, 6, 16, 18

caminar, 16

colmillos, 12

comida, 14, 16

jugar, 10

lodo, 8

madres, 18, 20

manadas, 20

noche, 20

pasto, 4, 14

piel, 8

quemadura de sol, 8

sabana, 4, 6, 16

trompas, 10, 14, 18